KIDS' QUICKEST
COMEBACKS

By **Matt Rissinger**
& **Philip Yates**

Illustrated by **Rob Collinet**

STERLING

New York / London
www.sterlingpublishing.com/kids

Library of Congress Cataloging-in-Publication Data Available

Rissinger, Matt.
Kids' quickiest comebacks / Matt Rissinger & Philip Yates ; illustrated
by Rob Collinet.
    p. cm.
  Includes index.
  ISBN 1-4027-0987-0
1. Wit and humor, Juvenile. 2. Invective--Juvenile humor. [1.Wit and
humor. 2. Invective--Humor.] I.Yates, Philip. II. Collinet, Rob, ill. III. Title.
  PN6166.R63 2004
  818'.6402--dc22
        2003024874

Lot #:
10 9 8 7 6 5 4 3
02/14
Published by Sterling Publishing Co., Inc.
387 Park Avenue South, New York, NY 10016

Distributed in Canada by Sterling Publishing
c/o Canadian Manda Group, 165 Dufferin Street
Toronto, Ontario, Canada M6K 3H6
Distributed in Australia by Capricorn Link (Australia) Pty. Ltd.
P.O. Box 704, Windsor, NSW 2756, Australia

Sterling ISBN 978-1-4027-7851-3

For information about custom editions, special sales, premium and
corporate purchases, please contact Sterling Special Sales
Department at 800-805-5489 or specialsales@sterlingpublishing.com.

CONTENTS

BE A COMEBACK KID!

How many times have you walked away from a really stupid question and asked yourself: "Why didn't I think of a clever comeback?"

Well, walk away no more, because this book contains hundreds of quick comebacks for every situation imaginable—well, almost every situation imaginable—like when your teacher asks you:

Why are you always daydreaming in science class?

Most of us would shake ourselves awake and mutter an apology. But if you have the makings of a true Comeback Kid, you might respond robustly:

I'm trying to come up with a formula to make homework disappear.

Or:

- ✌ I'm not daydreaming. I'm holding a séance with the souls of dearly departed dissected frogs.
- ✌ Science class! No wonder I can't find my place in this social studies book.
- ✌ Daydreaming? What gave me away—the pillow or the alarm clock?

A quick, clever comeback will not only make you proud, but win you many friends who will applaud your wit, salute your sarcasm, and bow to your brilliance.

They'll also be in awe of your courage for standing up for yourself while you're being led away to detention.

No, wait—*stop the dream sequence*—not detention! Let's rewind. There's a time and a place for clever comebacks, and what's the point of getting into trouble with your favorite teacher? Use your comebacks wisely and discreetly and at the right place and the right time.

Like right now. Memorize enough of these potent antidotes, and when an irritating interrogative comes your way, you'll never catch another case of **stupid-questionitis.**

Good luck, and welcome to the world where Comeback Kids rule!

1. LET'S NOT GET PERSONAL!

Where are your manners?

Manners! I thought you said banan-ners. Are you trying to make a monkey out of me?

Hmm, . . . I love a good mystery, don't you?

I'm not sure, but I found a frog in my pocket yesterday.

I don't know. Have you checked the lost and found?

Let's look for yours first, then maybe mine will show up, too.

Are those your clothes?

Yes, I gave them to charity, but they gave them back.

Yes, I shop at Dumpsters 'R' Us.

Yes, they're 100% natural fiber...made from authentic South Dakota buffalo chips.

No, they're just loaners from the prison laundry.

Yes—do you know how many polyesters were sacrificed to make this shirt?

No, actually I'm naked—what you see is a holographic projection.

Do you like them? They've been in the family for ages. Actually, since the Middle Ages.

No, it's a Roman toga I borrowed from the Museum of Ancient History.

Are you taking a bath?

Yes, I think I'll take it to the movies.

No, I'm reenacting the final scene from the Titanic.

No, I'm practicing synchronized swimming for the Olympics.

No, I'm exercising my rubber ducky.

No, the girls all say I look cute in dirt.

No, I'm just studying for my plumber's final exam.

No, but if I stay in here another hour I'll have enough wrinkles to be a raisin for Halloween.

No, I'm marinating myself for the big Cannibal Cookout.

Are those really your own ears?

No, they're satellite dishes. I get nearly 500 clear channels.

Yes, and I can swat flies with them, too.

No, I'm auditioning for *Dumbo, the Miniseries.*

No, two miniature flying saucers crashed into the sides of my head.

Yes, everyone on my home planet, Vulcan, has them.

No, I use these to go hang-gliding.

Yes, when I was cloned there was some elephant DNA left in the test tube.

No, they're just photo doubles. I keep my real ears at home.

Why are you sucking your thumb?

My mom forgot to pack my lunch today.

This is how I inflate the rest of my body.

It's the only way I found to remove that black dirt from under the nail.

Because I nearly broke my neck sucking my big toe.

My other fingers were busy.

Because hitchhikers need to look clean.

Because I don't know where *your* thumb has been.

My mom's out of town, so I have to baby myself.

Are you really that short?

No, I'm trying out for a part in *Honey, I Shrunk the Kids II*.

Yes, do you want to see my actual growth chart? It's printed on the back of this matchbook.

Yes, that's why I need a ladder to get over the curb.

No, this is my Halloween costume. I'm going as a Popsicle stick.

No. Try turning your binoculars around and looking at me again.

2. SNAPPY SNIPPY REPLIES

Are those peppers too hot?

Compared to the sun, no.

Peppers? Oh thank goodness. For a minute I thought I swallowed a Bunsen burner.

No, but I could use some rocket fuel to cool off.

It depends. Which end is the smoke supposed to come out of?

No. I'm working on my fire-starter scout badge and now I use my breath instead of two sticks.

Is that your new bowling ball?

No, it's the world's biggest marble.

No, it's a three-holed hamster habitat.

No, it's King Kong's ping-pong ball.

No, it's the world's biggest wad of used chewing gum.

No, it's a big, brash bran muffin intent on taking over the world.

No, it's my new cell phone—put your ear to it and listen to the calls come rolling in.

Is that your water bottle?

No, that's an aquarium for my invisible fish collection.

No, it's my new invention—see-through milk.

No, it's a bottle of eyewash for my pet Cyclops.

No, I was running late today, so I had to pack a portable shower.

Yes, my class voted me Home Room Fireman.

Did you catch that fish?

No, this fish said he'd rather be in my boat than in a school.

No, he surrendered voluntarily.

No, I was sitting here minding my own business when the crazy thing fell from the sky.

Yes, I caught him. Want to hear him sing and move his mouth?

No, it's a plastic model to get people like you to start conversations.

No, this clever worm caught him.

No, this is a flying fish. He just stopped here to rest on his way south for the winter.

Yes, I didn't have a date for the junior prom and this looked like a good catch.

Are you wearing a Walkman?

No, this is the newest fad—audio earrings.

No, it's a cranial compass that keeps my head pointed toward the Magnetic North Pole.

No, this is a device that helps me walk and chew gum at the same time.

No, but it comes in handy when your parents ask you to do your chores.

Walkman? These are my supersonic ear cleaners.

No, it seems I have a fuzzy black fungus growing around my ears.

No, this is a dweeb alert system. Shhh! I think it is going off.

Can you repeat that? I can't hear you when I'm wearing a Walkman.

No, it's a coin detector. Do you mind throwing down a couple of quarters so I can test it?

Are those crutches?

No, these are devices to help soak up all the sweat from my armpits.

No, I'm a spy for the CIA and these are secret weapons.

No, they're matching toothpicks for the Jolly Green Giant.

No, I'm searching for hidden treasure and these are my twin metal detectors.

No, these are giant wishbones from an overgrown turkey. Wanna make a wish?

No, they're retro rocket fire packs. I can zoom from class to recess in nanoseconds.

No, they're leftover chopsticks from a giant Chinese dinner.

No, they're my new invention—twin pogo sticks.

Why are you standing on your head?

My feet are
tired.

My nose is
running.

I hear this is
the best way
to get cable TV
reception.

I forgot to
wear a belt
and this is
the only way
I know to
keep my
pants up.

I just ironed
my pants and
now I'm
working on
pressing my
hair.

I want to
touch the sky,
and my legs
are longer
than my arms.

3. IT'S QUIPPING TIME!

How did the house get so neat?

I turned the oven on "automatic clean" and left the door open.

I propped the windows open during last night's windstorm.

Hypnosis. When I snap my fingers, you'll see a mess again.

Some burglars must have cleaned us out.

We're in the wrong house.

Is this elevator going up?

No, this elevator's going "ding."

No, it only goes down. What button should I push—China?

This isn't an elevator—it's a test track for flying squirrels.

No, this elevator goes side to side. Next stop—the near horizon.

This isn't an elevator—it's a closet with music.

This isn't an elevator. It's the world's largest microwave oven.

Are you trying to push my buttons?

Elevator? Didn't you see the sign—NASA Launching Pad?

Did you cut your finger?

Yes, I'm trying to bait a vampire.

Ever hear of DNA? It stands for "DO NOT ASK"!

No, but I have a whole box of Band-Aids that are about to expire and I have to use them up.

No, my finger prefers to cut itself, thank you.

No, it's ketchup just in case I'm attacked by a French fry.

No, it's just a simple computer byte.

Why are you making that clicking noise?

I accidentally swallowed my computer mouse.

I'm learning how to speak Dolphin.

Sorry, it's my heels. I keep clicking them so I'll end up back in Kansas.

I must have put in the wrong teeth today.

This is how I communicate with the Mother Ship.

Why aren't you going into the swimming pool?

My bathing suit isn't waterproof.

There aren't enough piranhas in there to satisfy my sense of adventure.

I might get wet.

My battery-powered bathing cap might short out.

The chlorine doesn't taste as good as it used to.

I'm so thin I might get sucked through the drain hole!

I'm waiting for the Loch Ness Monster to clear out.

There've been reports of enemy submarines in the area.

There's a full moon rising, and I wouldn't want to be swimming with wet werewolves.

Are you laughing at me?

No, I just opened up my report card.

I'm not laughing. I'm having an anxiety attack. Give me some air!

Sorry, seeing one of those "KICK ME" signs always makes me chuckle.

No, my imaginary playmate just told me a great joke.

4. WISH I'D SAID THAT!

What took you so long to come for dinner?

I lost the map to the kitchen.

I was trying to get the taste out of my mouth from breakfast.

I was searching through the medicine cabinet for a good poison antidote.

I was waiting until the dog taste-tested it first.

I was filing my incisors to a point to chew through the meat loaf.

I heard we were having Baked Alaska, so I've been rummaging around to find some snow shoes.

You aren't afraid of shots, are you?

Well, when you said "Get a booster," I thought you meant a higher cushion.

Ghosts, zombies, mummies, no. Shots, yes.

It depends on who's calling them.

I don't mind the shots, but the sight of cotton balls makes me faint.

Only if it's hunting season and I'm dressed up like
Daffy Duck.

Why is it that every time I go to the doctor, I feel
like I'm on pins and needles?

If you want to draw blood, take an art class.

Why don't you take an X-ray instead? I prefer
snapshots, anyway.

Why is your room such a mess?

It's always like this after an alien abduction.

Two words—buffalo stampede.

My doctor says I'm allergic to cleanliness.

At least it's organized. Dirty underwear on that side, smelly socks on this side...

This room is my ticket to first place in the Science Fair Pollution Contest.

I'll turn the lights off. There, that's better.

Cleaning up means W-O-R-K, and you told me to stay away from four-letter words.

I'm collecting lint so I can make a quilt for the needy.

Blame gravity. I enjoy watching the dust particles float by.

What do you have to say about this terrible report card?

Yes, it is a mess, isn't it? I hate the color of the paper, and the graphics are much too busy.

Don't I have the right to remain silent?

Look on the bright side—at least I'm not cheating.

Next time I'll have to study harder or cheat better.

The "F" means Fantastic.

I got there late and all the ABCs were taken.

It's not a report card. It's a "Let's Get Grounded Announcement Card."

Well, at least you can recycle it.

You aren't going to leave the house wearing that?

I have to—all my nerdy clothes are in the wash.

Of course not, I'm just wearing this to the nude beach.

If you walk in front of me holding a leash, nobody will notice.

Leave? I'm just coming back.

As long as I have my Harry Potter invisibility cloak, who will know?

Don't worry; the police will have me back before curfew.

Don't worry; I'll wear my dark sunglasses so nobody will recognize me.

The good news: This is a reversible vest. The bad news: The other side is worse.

It's okay. I heard that the Fashion Police are busy investigating a Capri caper today.

Why are you always at the bottom of your class?

What does it matter? They teach the same subject at both ends.

I want to be an oceanographer when I grow up.

I love company. You know, it's lonely at the top.

I'm afraid of heights.

I'm a deep thinker.

Because from where I sit, everything's looking up.

5. SCHOOL FOOLERY

Why did you miss the bus this morning?

I didn't miss it. I plastered it with seven snowballs before it got away.

I'm scared of my bus driver. He was just voted Demolition Driver of the Year.

I didn't miss it. The bus narrowly missed me. Boy, was it close!

Someone moved the bus stop to a new time zone.

The ride is boring and it always goes to the same place.

What's your excuse for being out of school all week?

I'm a failure. My goal was to stay out all month.

Do you believe in alien abduction?

A thousand pardons…. I was bitten by a rattler, died, and just got reincarnated late last night.

My goldfish died and I had to bury him at sea.

Last Monday, I crawled into my locker to take a nap and the door locked behind me.

Do you have a number 2 pencil for the test?

No, I have a number 4 pencil; I thought I would just break it in half.

Why, what do you have to trade?

No, call me old-fashioned, but I have five feathers and an inkwell.

Oh, was that a pencil? I thought it was a seven-grain bread stick so I ate it.

I don't know. Let me chew on it a while.

For me I have a pencil. For the test I have a portable paper shredder.

Do you call this a book report?

No, I called it "QUITS" after I fell asleep.

No, I call it a waste of paper.

No, I call it Spot, but it doesn't seem to respond.

No, I call it a door stop—you can call it what you want.

I'm sorry, I'm beyond the name-calling stage.

No, you can use it as a paper hat, or as a sailboat....

No, it's my mid-morning snack. I'm partial to paper.

The website I copied it from claimed it was.

Did you just call out in class?

Yes, would you prefer I use my cell phone?

Yes, I was an auctioneer in a former life.

No, my imaginary playmate is a ventriloquist.

Sorry, I must have been talking in my sleep.

No, I think we may have stumbled on a natural echo outcropping.

It wasn't really a call out; it was more like a plea for mercy.

Why are you passing notes?

I don't know the e-mail address.

It's the only passing I'm going to be doing in this class.

My cell phone battery is dead.

It's not a note—it's our escape plan.

I forgot how to fold them into airplanes.

Are you going to detention?

Shhh! I'm really an undercover journalist doing a report on cruel and unusual punishment.

Yes, it's the only peace and quiet I get in school.

Yes, I missed it yesterday and I'm starting to suffer from detention deficit disorder.

Yes, it gives me a chance to figure out who I'm going to annoy tomorrow.

Yes, the teachers can't get enough of me.

On the down side, I don't like being cooped up. On the up side, I don't have to eat in the school cafeteria.

This isn't a detention slip—it's a personal invitation to the principal's surprise birthday party.

Why are you standing on your desk?

I didn't want to disturb the tarantula on my chair.

My counselor says I function best at a higher level.

I'm retrieving my pencil. It accidentally fell up through this ceiling tile.

My brain is overheating and I need to be close to the sprinkler system.

I'm scared of technology, and someone let loose a computer mouse.

I'm practicing for my tap dancing recital.

Isn't this gymnastics class?

I'm trying to scale new heights.

Is this the third time this week you've been late?

Yes, I'm finally getting it right.

Yes, nice of you to notice.

Since this is only Monday, I doubt it.

I'm sorry I can't talk now—I'm late.

My limo driver keeps getting lost.

6. BANTER UP!

Are you exercising?

No, I'm collecting sweat to send to under-privileged children in really cold climates.

No, I'm just breaking in these sneakers for a friend.

No, our neighborhood just installed a moving sidewalk.

No, I'm practicing running away from home.

No, a spider just crawled down my shorts and I'm trying to shake him out.

Why don't you want to come to your sister's music recital?

I have to be on the next train to Gilligan's Island.

I'm making a home movie called "The Thing That Grew and Grew in Our Refrigerator."

My yucca plant is feeling yucky, so I'm going to talk to it.

I never go out on days that end in "Y."

I just picked up a book called "Glue in Many Lands" and I can't put it down.

Somebody has to stay home and babysit the goldfish.

I'll wait until it comes out on DVD.

Because I haven't located my earplugs from her last recital.

I'm a big fan of music.

I'd like to hang out with you, but...

I have to finish my book called, "How to Lose a Friend in Five Days."

There's a disturbance in The Force.

I have to go to the post office to see if I'm still wanted.

I'm converting my calendar watch from Julian to Gregorian.

I promised to help a friend fold road maps.

I have to study for an eye test.

I have to stay home and rearrange my sock drawer.

I'm memorizing the phone book in case it gets misplaced.

Sorry, tomorrow night is a full moon and I have to scout howling locations.

I promised the CIA I would help them decode rap lyrics.

Why do you have such a big mouth?

So the school bus can have a place to park.

So I can eat a three-foot-long hot dog sideways.

So I can eat corn on the cob without using my fingers.

Because my dentist has such big hands.

So I can dub the screams in horror movies.

When the refrigerator is full, it's a nice place to store leftovers.

It's really handy when I'm juggling bowling balls.

I needed a portable cave habitat for my bat collection.

Are you teaching your dog to fetch?

No, I'm teaching this stick to fly.

That's not a dog—it's an anteater after a Hollywood nose job.

Yes, earlier I taught him quantum physics, and now we're moving on to something more challenging.

No, I'm seeing how much dog spit I can collect between my fingers.

No I'm just trying to get him to lose some weight so he can fit into his doghouse.

That's no dog—-that's my baby brother learning how to serve his older sibling.

No, I'm trying to teach him to pogo, but he keeps tumbling off the stick.

Yes, he's trying out for the Major Leagues next week.

No, he's teaching me how to toss this long thin object through that window.

Why do you have your nose in a book?

I forgot my handkerchief.

I'm too cheap to buy sun block.

It's a scratch-and-sniff story about the history of chocolate.

My nose can't read, so I borrowed someone else's.

It's a mystery and I'm sniffing out the suspect.

It's a polite way of ignoring people, but obviously it doesn't work for everyone.

Because yesterday it was my ear's turn.

I tried putting a book in my nose, but oddly I find that reversing the order is more delightful.

Are you going on a sleepover?

No, I'm on my way to class.

No, I'm spreading pillows and sleeping bags around the neighborhood to attract sleep-walkers.

No, I'm going to school dressed in my pajamas so everyone will make fun of me.

No, I thought I'd rob a mattress store in this getup.

No, to the library. We're reading selected scenes from *Goodnight Moon*.

This is my undercover spy outfit for the CIA.

7. OUTRAGEOUS CONTAGIOUS WISECRACKS

Are you going to karate class?

Let's just say we're going chopping!

No, we're celebrating National No Socks & Shoes Day.

No, these are my bed sheets in case a sleepover breaks out in math class.

No, I'm going to a Jackie Chan film festival.

No, we're all barefoot because we're off to a toenail paintin' party.

Are you using a glue stick?

No, this is lip balm for people who should know when to shut their mouths.

No, it's vanilla pop-up ice cream. Do you want a lick?

No, it's part of my wizard homework: snail slime in a tube.

No, the glue stick is using me. I am under its hypnotic power.

Yes, and it's gotten me out of plenty of sticky situations.

No, it's a new deodorant roll-on for Barbie dolls.

Yes—my computer is so old, I have to use this to copy and paste.

Glue stick! No wonder I can't get out any candy. I thought this was a Pez dispenser.

Is that your cat?

No, it's my pet monkey dressed up for Halloween.

No, my baby brother always coughs up hairballs.

No, that's a cougar that escaped from the zoo.

No, it's not my cat. I kidnapped him and I'm holding him for ransom.

No, it's Aunt Theresa reincarnated as a tabby.

No, it's our school mascot in disguise.

No, it's my new shape-shifting black sweater.

Yes, and if you're nice, he might let you play with his squeaky toy.

Are you going to the beach?

No, this is a giant tongue depressor I found on the highway.

No, I'm in the school band and this is our uniform.

No, this white stuff all over my body isn't suntan lotion—it's marshmallow cream.

No, I'm going to school dressed like this so I can be the first to see the school nurse.

No, the beaches are closed today, so I thought I'd go for a swim in the fountain at the mall.

Why don't you ever smile?

Every time I do my teeth fall out.

Oh, I do...but only when you're walking away.

I don't want to blind people with my dazzling whites.

I'm too lazy. Smiling involves exercising the muscles in your mouth.

Because you never know what's going to fly into your mouth.

I do smile. It's so quick you can't see it. There, I did it again.

Are you reading the back of that cereal box?

Yes, there's a special feature here on how to deal with stupid questions.

No, I'm just waiting until the Snap, Crackle, and Pop quiet down in my cereal.

Absolutely. How else would I figure out the Meaning of Life?

Shhh! I'm getting to the good part about Captain Crunch's dark years.

Yes, I'm trying to figure how much I have to eat to go into a sugar coma.

Yeah, I started reading it, but now I think I'll just wait until they turn it into a movie.

It may look like a cereal box, but it's really a stupid-question detector. Did you just hear it beep?

Absolutely not. What kind of a flake do you think I am?

Are you going somewhere with that suitcase?

This isn't a suitcase—it's my Uncle Harold. He's such a square.

Yes, I'm taking it to the airport so it can get lost real good.

You are so computer illiterate. This is the world's biggest laptop.

Freestyling! My skateboard is broken and this is the only thing I could find with wheels.

No, it lives in such a stuffy closet that I thought I'd take it out for some air.

No, this suitcase has a mind of its own and I don't know where it's taking me.

Help! Help! I'm being abducted by an alien from Planet Rectangle!

Keep your voice down—my little brother's been grounded and I'm trying to sneak him out to the movies.

Did you order a pizza?

No, I'm practicing for the discus throwing competition.

No, I think the dog ordered it…. But the cat is going to pay for it.

No, Mom did. After she hit that last pothole she needed a new hubcap.

No, but I'll use it for a prop in my new sci-fi movie "Attack of the Killer Anchovies."

No, it's a manhole cover with extra cheese.

Yes, stack it on top of the others. For history class I'm constructing the Leaning Tower of Pizza.

8. RETORTING FOR DUTY!

How did you finally make it out of third grade?

I got a senior citizen discount.

We had a fire drill.

I finally got good directions.

A spot opened up for me at Harvard.

I cloned myself, and he helped me with my homework.

I won the lottery and bought my own school.

Is that a hole in your pants?

No, it's a portal to a parallel universe.

I'm playing the role of Captain Underpants and wanted to work into the part slowly.

Hmm... I guess I'll have to mend my ways.

Oh, my gosh! My pet ferret just chewed his way to freedom!

Yes, it matches the one in your head.

Faked you out again—it's really a tattoo of a hole in my pants.

Yes, that's where I keep all the answers to tomorrow's test.

Are you putting up a birdhouse?

No, it's for squirrels. I call it a nuthouse.

No, it's a habitat for rich hamsters who want to live above their means.

No, it's a mailbox for passing pigeons.

No, my sister just bought Airline Barbie, and Barbie needs a place to land.

No, this is a secret castle for little gnome people.

No, I'm building a rocket ship that'll launch the first sparrow into space.

No, it's a telescope disguised as a birdhouse to spy on my neighbors.

No, it's a docking station for tiny alien aircraft.

Are you making toast?

No, it's my new invention—a suntan lamp for the Pillsbury Doughboy.

No, I'm making a grilled cheese sandwich minus the cheese.

No, my hair dryer is broken, so I'm using the toaster instead.

No, it's dark outside, so I turned this machine to "light," but I don't see any improvement.

No, I'm torturing sliced bread.

Yes, they make great coasters if you let them sit for a while.

No, the heater is broken, and I'm warming up the house.

No, I'm practicing my batting. Every time a slice pops up I whack it with a bread stick.

Are you replacing those batteries?

No, I find it more economical to keep the batteries and throw away the radio.

No, I'm just reversing their polarity in case the world starts spinning backward.

No, I'm taking them to my secret laboratory to jump-start a monster brain.

Yes, my baby brother is really a robot.

No, these are packs of Lifesavers—they're so colorful and seem to work better than batteries.

Are you guys building a soapbox derby car?

No, we're building the world's wackiest paperweight.

No, we're building a birdhouse for Road Runner.

No, we're filming a Home Depot commercial.

No, we were building a nuclear submarine, but we ran low on enriched uranium.

No, we're building a traveling termite trailer.

Are you waiting for Santa?

Santa? I thought this was the line for Dallas Cowboy Cheerleader autographs.

No, I'm waiting to grow taller so I can apply for a job as an elf.

No, I'm just here for a photo opportunity. I was absent on school picture day.

Yes, and my wish this year is not to have to stand in line next year.

No, I'm waiting to talk to my doctor; he's the third elf on the left.

No, Weight Watchers wants me to have a word with the big guy in the red suit about cutting back on the milk and cookies.

Yes, Rudolph isn't returning my e-mails.

No, I'm from the Department of Health. We're fining that jolly joker for excessive reindeer droppings.

No, I'm with Ajax Janitorial. We're just waiting for the crowd to clear out so we can clean the carpets.

Is that a hula hoop?

Hula hoop! I thought it was a new belt. No wonder I can't get it through my pant loops.

No, I'm learning how to throw my back out.

No, I'm reenacting the Circle of Life dance from the Lion King.

No, it's King Kong's toe ring.

No, I'm a fallen angel and I'm trying to work this halo back over my head.

No, Godzilla had her belly button pierced and I'm delivering her ring.

Am I boring you?

No—I'm not yawning. I'm just stretching my mouth.

No, these toothpicks are under my eyelids to attract woodpeckers.

I'm not yawning. It's a silent scream.

Wake me in a half-hour and I'll tell you.

I'm practicing opening my mouth wide for the dentist.

No, just because I'm covered in cobwebs doesn't mean you've been talking too long.

ABOUT THE AUTHORS

Matt lives near Valley Forge, Pennsylvania, with his wife, Maggie; his daughters, Rebecca, Emily, and Abigail; and their black Lab, Breaker. Philip lives in Austin, Texas, with his wife, Maria, and his cats Sam and Johnnie.

Philip and Matt's other Sterling books include *The Great Book of Zany Jokes, The Biggest Joke Book in the World, World's Silliest Jokes, Best School Jokes Ever, Greatest Jokes on Earth, Totally Terrific Jokes, Giggle Fit: Nutty Jokes, Giggle Fit: Wacky Jokes, Greatest Giggles Ever, It's Not My Fault: Kids' Excuse Book,* and *Greatest Kids' Comebacks Ever.*

ABOUT THE ILLUSTRATOR

Rob lives in Toronto, Canada, with his wife, Karen; his son, Hobbes; Marty, their Boston Terrier; and Seetz, their cat.

Rob's other Sterling books include *Totally Silly Jokes, Super Goofy Jokes,* and *Challenging Logic Puzzles.*

INDEX